Happy Birthday to a lovely WIFE

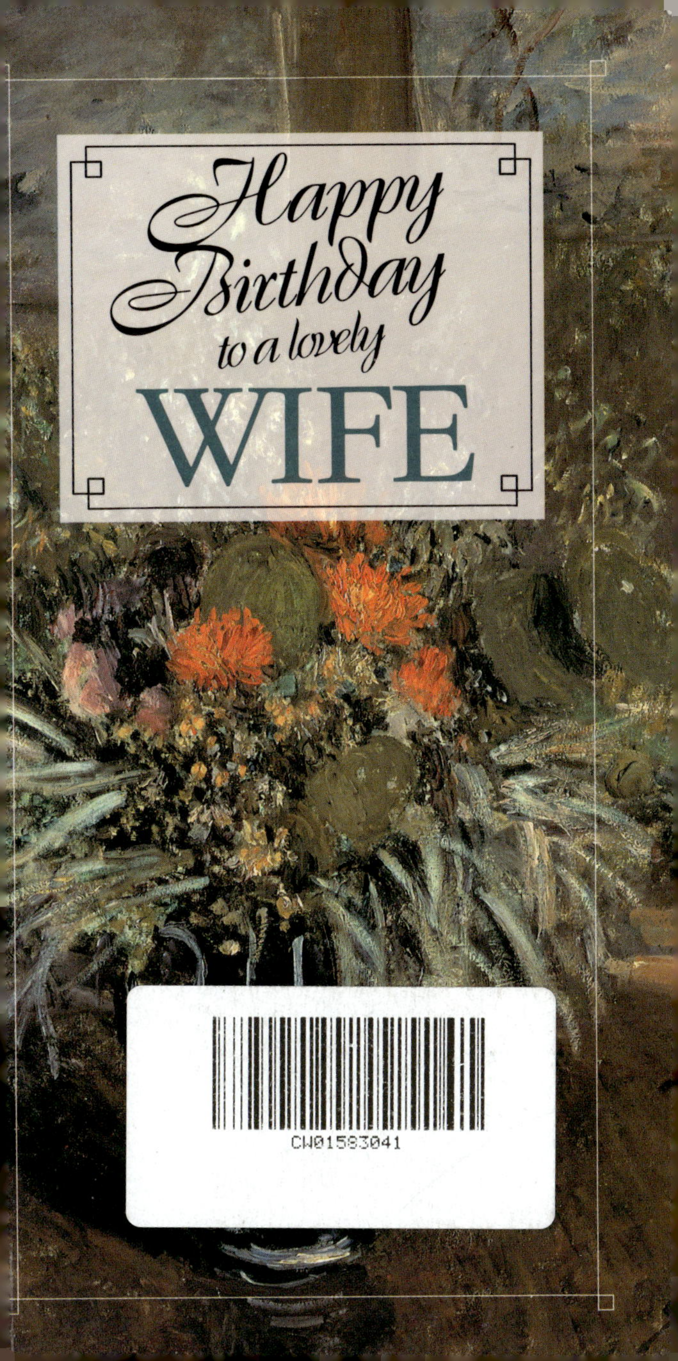

To my special wife –
enjoy your special day!
Have the happiest of birthdays,
and together let us make this the
very best of years!

To:

From:

Sisley.

This birthday I give you a
present – as I always do when
I've not been muddled and
forgotten! But you defeat me –
for you've given me a gift beyond
all price. Yourself.
A parcel packed all neat and nice
with loving, kindness, smiles....

Husbands are very often not good at showing what they feel. "That's nice" they say. And "What have you done to your hair?" And "You passed? I knew you would."
So, on this special day, I want to say all the things I ought to have said long before. With all my love.

A wife brings many gifts – but more than pies and puddings, mended socks, the kindly trivia of everyday – she brings herself.
An everchanging landscape.
A woman capable of miracles: of love and strength.

Once we stood facing one another – seeing only love; but now we stand side by side, companions, lovers, friends – and so can share the world. Seas, stars and trees have been transformed by shared delight – and we are part of them.

Reason tells me you must have
changed – and in old
photographs you look
ridiculously young! – Yet when
I'm with you I can see
no alteration worth the mention.
You are still the young woman
that took my heart and held it.

My days are so full of travel,
talk, decisions, small and great,
the clutter of a working week –
no one would think that I have
time to spare for other thoughts.
How wrong they are! You are
always there – like the beating of
my heart.

You are so much a part of my life. I look about me – your touch is everywhere. You are entwined in everything I say or do. Your heartbeat, your gentle breathing, your words, your smiles, pervade my being. Your absence diminishes me.

You have taught me to experience the world through your senses as well as through my own – and so I have discovered unsuspected wonders.

Thank you – for all you've brought into my life. Before I knew you I was only half alive.

Every living thing must grow and change or die. And so must love. Each gale, each bitter frost will leave its mark. Each drought each glorious summer and each spring will lend new strength and new growth.
And so our love renews itself.

Forgive me if, obsessed with my own concerns, I've shut you out. All day I've had to wear a mask and only as I shut the door behind me can I let it fall. Forgive me. Understand. Be patient. You are my peace, my reassurance.

I stand and face the mirror
and I sigh. I pull my
stomach in. Throw out my
chest.
Hopeless.
When everything has
shifted, the inner structure
skewed, the outer slumped
– I wonder sometimes how
you go on loving me.
But then I see you grin.
Disintegration treats us
both equally. How lucky
that we've learned to
recognize the people
underneath the skin.

To love you was once simple –
for I saw the girl I needed in
your face. But every year
has taught me more about you –
and all I learn has made me love
you more. I think I never will
discover all there is to learn.
Or ever cease to love.

Funny face. I love each line, each quirk, each oddity. I love your laugh, your silly habits, your tricks of speech, each frailty, each flaw. Along with all your virtues. For I love you entire – the whole bewilderment of you. Astonish me for ever!

HAPPY BIRTHDAY TO A LOVELY WIFE
From the SO-MUCH-MORE-THAN-A-CARD™ collection by Exley Publications
PAINTINGS BY ALFRED SISLEY (1839-1899)
WRITTEN BY PETER GRAY
EDITED BY HELEN EXLEY
Published simultaneously in 1996 by Exley Giftbooks in the USA and Exley Publications Ltd in Great Britain.
12 11 10 9 8 7 6 5 4 3 2

ISBN 1-85015-716-2

Typeset by Delta, Watford.
Printed and bound by Graficas Reunidas SA, Madrid, Spain.
Picture Credits: The publishers would like to thank the following organizations for permission to reproduce their pictures: Art Resource (AR) and Bridgeman Art Library (BAL). Cover and Envelope: Still Life of Flowers (BAL); page 1: The Small Meadows in Spring, 1880, Tate Gallery (AR); page 3: L'Ile Saint Denis, 1872 (AR); page 5: In the Vineyards at Louveciennes (BAL); page 7: View of the Canal Saint-Martin, 1870 (AR); page 9: Path Leading to Ville d'Avray, 1879 (BAL); page 11: Bridge of Moret-sur-Loing, 1887, (BAL); page 13: Louveciennes, 1873 (BAL); page 15: Moret-sur-Loing, 1891 (BAL); page 17: Port Marly, White Frost, 1872 (AR); page 19: Village by the Seine, 1876, Hermitage Museum, St. Petersburg (BAL); page 21: View of the Sevres Road (BAL); page 23: Canal du Loing at Moret (AR); page 25: A corner of the woods at Sablons, 1883 (AR).
EXLEY PUBLICATIONS LTD, 16 CHALK HILL, WATFORD, HERTS WD1 4BN, UK.
EXLEY GIFTBOOKS, 232 MADISON AVENUE, SUITE 1206, NY 10016, USA.

Paintings by
ALFRED SISLEY
Birthday messages for wives

FROM THE EXLEY PUBLICATIONS
SO-MUCH-MORE-THAN-A-CARD™ COLLECTION

EXLEY
NEW YORK • WATFORD, UK

ISBN 1-85015-716-2

9 781850 157168

UK£1.99 US$2.99